DOWN-HOME COOKING

Pure Wesson®

IT'S COOKIN' TIME

PUBLICATIONS INTERNATIONAL, LTD.

Copyright © 1997 Publications International, Ltd.
Recipes and text copyright © 1997 Hunt-Wesson, Inc.
All rights reserved. This publication may not be reproduced or quoted in whole or in part by any means whatsoever without written permission from:

Louis Weber, CEO
Publications International, Ltd.
7373 North Cicero Avenue
Lincolnwood, Illinois 60646

Permission is never granted for commercial purposes.

Wesson and Peter Pan are registered trademarks of Hunt-Wesson, Inc. Fullerton, California 92633-3899. Knott's Berry Farm is a registered trademark of Knott's Berry Farm licensed to Hunt-Wesson Foods.

Wesson Cookbook Project Manager: Lena Mercurio-Cutler
Wesson Test Kitchen Senior Home Economist: Lena Mercurio-Cutler
Wesson Test Kitchen Home Economists: Anita Dillon, Rhonda Mayo, Donna Malbon, Sharon Benson, Virginia Evans
Wesson Technical Photography Advisors: Lena Mercurio-Cutler, Carolyn Avelino
Wesson Clerical Coordinator: Betty Allen
Wesson Marketing: Michelle Corrigan

Photography: Sanders Studio, Inc., Chicago
Photographer: Kathy Sanders
Photography Assistants: Cristin Nestor, Kathy Ores
Prop Stylist: Patty Higgins
Food Stylists: Teri Rys-Maki, Diane Hugh
Assistant Food Stylists: Laura Hess

Pictured on the front cover: Buttermilk Ranch Fried Chicken *(page 58)*, mixed greens salad with Mrs. Farfsing's "One Dressing Fits All" *(page 30)* and Lickety-Split Beer Rolls *(page 19)*.

Preparation/Cooking Times: Preparation times are based on the approximate amount of time required to assemble the recipe before cooking, baking, chilling or serving. These times include preparation steps such as measuring, chopping and mixing. The fact that some preparations and cooking can be done simultaneously is taken into account. Preparation of optional ingredients and serving suggestions is not included.

ISBN: 0-7853-2396-1

Manufactured in U.S.A.

8 7 6 5 4 3 2 1

DOWN-HOME COOKING

Pure Wesson®

IT'S COOKIN' TIME

Introduction

We always say that at our next house we're going to knock out the living room and the dining room and just have one big kitchen, since that's where everyone always ends up anyway. Sometimes it seems our whole life is spent in that kitchen—telling stories, discussing problems, laughing and crying.

Cooking is a celebration and I put my heart into every meal. Nothing makes me prouder than seeing a bunch of happy faces around the table digging into one of my home cooked meals. That is why I'm happy to introduce this cookbook full of mouthwatering recipes from the Wesson Test Kitchen and Wesson Cookers' Club Recipe Contest Winners. You'll be proud to serve these family-pleasing recipes to your own family. If you feel as I do, it's the best way there is to tell them how much you love them.

Jo Ann Anthony, Harahan, Louisiana
1996 Wesson Cookers' Club Recipe Contest Winner
Spicy Fried Potatoes & Seasoned Fried Fish (page 76)
and Crawfish Egg Rolls (page 77)

Wesson's Hot Tips for Frequent Fryers

Get Ready

•It's Cookin' Time! Tune in to your favorite radio station and get ready for the celebration to begin!

•Set out the equipment you'll need for frying before you get started. This would include a deep-fry or candy thermometer to monitor the oil temperature, a slotted spoon or tongs for lifting food in and out of the oil and paper towels for blotting.

•Fill the deep-fry pot to no more than half its depth with Wesson Oil. Heat the oil to the required temperature. If you are using an electric skillet, you can set the temperature easily. If you are frying on your stove top, use your deep-fry thermometer to monitor the oil temperature and adjust the heat to maintain the correct temperature.

Preparing Foods for Frying

•Whether frying vegetables, fish or meat, the food you are preparing should be uniform in size. Similar sizes ensure that all food will fry in the same length of time.

- Raw or wet foods should be patted dry before frying to prevent oil from splattering.
- Don't crowd the food! Fry food in small batches. Overloading the pan will bring the oil temperature down and prevent even browning.

Let's Talk about Oil

- Most food fries between 325°F and 375°F. If your oil is smoking, the temperature is too high. Use an oil with a high smoke point such as Wesson Vegetable, Canola, Corn or Best Blend Oils, which are all excellent frying oils with smoke points well above 400°F.

- When deep-frying, there must be enough oil to cover the food and still be enough room in the pot to allow for easy movement of food.
- When the oil is at the correct temperature, the surface of the food will form a quick crust and less oil will be absorbed into the food.
- If you are frying different types of food, always fry the food with the strongest flavor and odor last.
- If used oil is dark brown or if it smells or tastes rancid, throw it out. Place it in a covered container and toss it in the trash. Never pour oil down the drain because it will clog the pipes.

Safety Tips

- Keep a box of baking soda close by in case of fire. If possible, try and cover the skillet or deep-fry pot with a lid to extinguish or contain the fire. NEVER THROW WATER ON AN OIL FIRE.
- Always use a large enough deep-fry pot or skillet for frying. Never fill the deep-fry pot to more than half its depth with oil.
- NEVER leave hot oil unattended.

One Last Tip

- ALWAYS fry twice as much of everything! Once your neighbors notice the delicious aromas coming from your kitchen, they will find any excuse to invite themselves over to your house!

Recipe Notations

Treat your family to delicious home-cooked meals with recipes that are designed to help you when you are short on time.

 Indicates recipes prepared from start to finish in 30 minutes or less.

 Indicates recipes prepared from start to finish in 45 minutes or less.

Breads & Muffins

*There is nothing like waking up to the aroma of
fresh baked muffins and breads.
Whip up one of these recipes and watch
your family spring out of bed!*

Peach Orchard Muffins

Wesson® No-Stick Cooking Spray
**1 (16-ounce) can sliced peaches in heavy syrup, diced,
    syrup reserved**
⅓ cup Wesson® Vegetable Oil
2 eggs, slightly beaten
1 teaspoon vanilla
2 cups all-purpose flour
⅓ cup sugar
3 teaspoons baking powder
½ teaspoon salt
½ cup Knott's Berry Farm® Peach Preserves
Sugar for topping

Preheat oven to 400°F. Spray 12 muffin cups with Wesson Cooking Spray.
In a small bowl, combine syrup, Wesson Oil, eggs and vanilla; mix well.
In a large bowl, mix together flour, sugar, baking powder and salt. Pour
egg mixture into flour mixture; stir just until dry ingredients are moistened.
Fold in diced peaches. Fill muffin cups to rim. Bake for 15 to 22 minutes
or until wooden pick inserted into center comes out clean. Cool 5 minutes.
Remove muffins to wire racks. Brush with Knott's preserves and
sprinkle with desired amount of sugar.   *Makes 1 dozen muffins*

*On plate: Strawberry-Patch Streusel
Muffins (page 11)
In basket: Peach Orchard Muffins, Calico
Spice Muffins (page 10) and Strawberry-
Patch Streusel Muffins (page 11)*

Calico Spice Muffins

Wesson® No-Stick Cooking Spray
2 cups all-purpose flour
¾ cup packed brown sugar
2½ teaspoons baking soda
2 teaspoons ground cinnamon
½ teaspoon salt
½ teaspoon nutmeg
½ teaspoon allspice
½ cup Wesson® Vegetable or Canola Oil
½ cup milk
3 eggs, beaten
2 teaspoons vanilla
2 cups grated carrots
2 cups peeled, cored and diced apples (Pippin, Granny
    Smith or Rome Beauty)
⅔ cup toasted coconut
⅔ cup toasted sliced almonds
⅔ cup raisins

Preheat oven to 375°F. Spray muffin cups with Wesson Cooking Spray. In a large bowl, combine *next* 7 ingredients, ending with allspice. In another bowl, stir together Wesson Oil, milk, eggs and vanilla; mix well. Gradually stir egg mixture into flour mixture until moistened. Fold in the *remaining* ingredients. Fill muffin cups to rim. Bake for 25 minutes or until wooden pick inserted into center comes out clean. Cool 5 minutes. Remove muffins to wire racks. Serve muffins warm or cool.

Makes 1½ dozen muffins

Toasted coconut adds a crunchy texture and a nutty flavor to these muffins. To toast coconut, spread coconut evenly on a baking sheet. Bake in 350°F oven for 3 minutes. Stir and bake 1 to 2 minutes longer or until light golden brown.

Strawberry-Patch Streusel Muffins

Wesson® No-Stick Cooking Spray

Topping:
 ¼ **cup chopped pecans**
 ¼ **cup packed brown sugar**
 ¼ **cup all-purpose flour**
 2 **tablespoons margarine or butter, melted**

Muffins:
 ¾ **cup milk**
 ⅔ **cup Wesson® Vegetable Oil**
 2 **eggs**
1½ **tablespoons grated fresh orange peel**
 2 **cups all-purpose flour**
 ⅓ **cup sugar**
 1 **tablespoon baking powder**
 ½ **teaspoon salt**
1½ **cups chopped strawberries *or* 1 cup chopped frozen**
     strawberries, thawed

Preheat oven to 400°F. Spray muffin cups with Wesson Cooking Spray.

Topping: In a small bowl, combine *all* ingredients for streusel topping; set aside.

Muffins: In a large bowl, combine milk, Wesson Oil, eggs and orange peel; mix well. In a large bowl, mix together flour, sugar, baking powder and salt. Pour egg mixture into flour mixture; stir just until dry ingredients are moistened. Fold in strawberries. Fill muffin cups to rim with batter. Sprinkle generously with streusel topping. Bake 10 to 20 minutes or until wooden pick inserted into center comes out clean. Cool 5 minutes. Remove muffins from pan; cool on wire rack.

Makes 1 dozen muffins

Because frozen strawberries are not as firm as fresh, the batter will turn pink when frozen strawberries are added.

Southern Caramel Pecan Rolls

Topping:
  ⅔ **cup sifted powdered sugar**
  ⅔ **cup dark brown sugar**
  ½ **cup whipping cream**
  1 **teaspoon vanilla**
     Wesson® No-Stick Cooking Spray
  1 **cup coarsely chopped pecans**

Rolls:
  1 **cup dark raisins**
  ⅓ **cup brandy**
  2 **(1-pound) loaves frozen sweet or white bread dough,**
     thawed, but not doubled in size
  ¼ **cup Wesson® Best Blend Oil**
  ½ **cup packed dark brown sugar**
  1 **tablespoon ground cinnamon**
  ½ **teaspoon ground nutmeg**

Topping: In a medium bowl, stir together sugars, whipping cream and vanilla. Spray two 9×1½-inch round cake pans with Wesson Cooking Spray. Evenly divide mixture into pans and sprinkle with pecans; set aside pans.

Rolls: In a small bowl, soak raisins in brandy for 30 minutes; set aside and stir occasionally.

On a floured surface, roll *each* loaf into a 12×8×¼-inch rectangle. Generously brush *each* sheet of dough with Wesson Oil. In a small bowl, mix together sugar, cinnamon and nutmeg. Sprinkle over dough; top with soaked raisins. Roll up rectangles jelly-roll style starting with the long edge. Pinch dough to seal. Cut into 12 slices. Place rolls, spiral side down, in cake pans. Cover with towels and let rise in a warm place for 30 minutes or until nearly double in size. Preheat oven to 375°F. Bake, uncovered, for 15 to 20 minutes. Cover pans with foil to prevent overbrowning and bake an additional 10 minutes. Cool in pans 7 minutes. Invert onto serving plate. Best when served warm.

Makes 24 rolls

Holiday Cranberry Pumpkin Bread

Wesson® No-Stick Cooking Spray

Bread:
2¼ cups sugar
　1 cup canned or cooked fresh pumpkin
　⅔ cup Wesson® Canola Oil
　2 eggs, lightly beaten
　1 tablespoon vanilla
2¼ cups all-purpose flour
　1 cup chopped walnuts or hazelnuts (optional)
　1 tablespoon pumpkin pie spice
　1 teaspoon baking soda
　½ teaspoon salt
　2 cups coarsely chopped fresh cranberries

Glaze:
1¼ cups powdered sugar
　2 to 3 tablespoons warmed milk
　⅔ cup coarsely chopped cranberries

Arrange rack in the middle of the oven. Preheat oven to 350°F. Spray two 8½×4½×2-inch loaf pans or one Bundt pan with Wesson Cooking Spray.

Bread: In medium bowl, combine sugar, pumpkin, Wesson Oil, eggs and vanilla; mix well. In large mixing bowl, combine *remaining* bread ingredients *except* cranberries. Make a well in the center of the flour mixture; pour pumpkin mixture into the center. Using a wooden spoon, slowly blend flour mixture with pumpkin mixture. Mix until dry ingredients are moistened. Fold cranberries into batter; spoon into pans. Bake for 1 hour or until wooden pick inserted into center comes out clean. Let bread cool 10 minutes on wire rack before removing from pan. Cool completely.

Glaze: In small bowl, combine sugar and milk; mix until smooth. Fold ⅓ *cup* cranberries into glaze. Place bread on wire rack with wax paper under rack. Spoon glaze over bread to completely cover tops. Sprinkle *remaining* cranberries on top of glaze. Let glaze dry at least 20 minutes before serving. 　　　　　*Makes 2 loaves or 1 Bundt bread*

Fanfare Dinner Rolls

1 cup warm water (105°F to 115°F)
2 envelopes quick-rising dry yeast
¼ teaspoon sugar
⅔ cup whole milk, room temperature
⅓ cup sugar
¼ cup Wesson® Canola Oil
1 large egg
1 tablespoon poppy seeds
2½ teaspoons salt
5⅓ cups all-purpose flour
1 cup (2 sticks) chilled unsalted butter, cut into thin slices
    Wesson® No-Stick Cooking Spray
3 tablespoons unsalted butter, melted
    Poppy seeds

Pour water into a large bowl. Sprinkle yeast, then *¼ teaspoon* sugar into water; stir well. Let stand 5 to 8 minutes or until mixture is slightly foamy. Meanwhile, in a small bowl, whisk milk, *⅓ cup* sugar, Wesson Oil, egg, poppy seeds and salt until well blended. Pour milk mixture into yeast mixture; mix well. Gradually add *1 cup* flour to mixture and stir until batter is smooth. In a food processor, combine *4 cups* flour and chilled butter; process until mixture resembles a coarse meal. Add to batter and stir until dry ingredients are moistened. Knead dough in bowl (about 5 minutes) until smooth. Add more flour if dough is sticky. Cover with towels and let rise in a warm place for 30 minutes or until dough nearly doubles in size.

Spray 24 muffin cups with Wesson Cooking Spray. Turn dough onto floured surface; knead about 4 minutes until dough is smooth and elastic. Evenly divide dough into 4 portions. Place *1 portion* on floured surface; cover and refrigerate *remaining* portions. Roll dough to 13×12×⅛-inch rectangle. Cut rectangle lengthwise into six 2-inch strips. Stack strips *on top of each other* to form *6 layers*. Cut stack into *6 equal* individual small stacks. Place *each* stack, cut side down, into muffin cup. Repeat with *remaining* dough sections. Cover with a towel; let rise in a warm place for 30 minutes or until nearly doubled in size.

continued on page 18

Fanfare Dinner Rolls

Fanfare Dinner Rolls, continued

Position one rack in the center of oven and the other rack above the first, allowing plenty of space for rolls to continue rising while baking. Preheat oven to 350°F. Brush rolls gently with melted butter; sprinkle with poppy seeds. Bake for 25 minutes until golden brown. Switch muffin pans halfway through bake time. Cool rolls 7 to 10 minutes. Remove rolls from pan; cool on wire rack. Serve warm.

Makes 2 dozen rolls

If you have any leftover dough, roll it into balls. Roll each ball lightly in Wesson Oil and cinnamon-sugar. Place on a cookie sheet and bake until golden brown.

Melt-in-Your-Mouth Boston Brown Bread

Judy Tenny
Waxhaw, North Carolina
1996 Wesson Cookers' Club Recipe Contest Winner

Wesson® No-Stick Cooking Spray
1 cup sugar
½ cup Wesson® Canola Oil
½ cup molasses
2 eggs, beaten
2 cups all-purpose flour
2 teaspoons baking soda
1 teaspoon salt
1 cup boiling water

Preheat oven to 350°F. Spray a 9×5×2-inch loaf pan with Wesson Cooking Spray. In a large mixing bowl, with electric mixer, cream together sugar, Wesson Oil, molasses and eggs at MEDIUM speed. In a small bowl, blend flour, baking soda and salt together; mix well. Gradually add egg mixture to flour mixture; mix well. Reduce mixer speed to LOW; add water and mix well. Spoon batter into pan. Bake for 45 to 50 minutes or until wooden pick inserted into center comes out clean. Cool 10 minutes. Remove bread from pan; cool on wire rack.

Makes 1 loaf

Judy serves this bread alongside a bowl of hot soup, with a fancy meal for dinner parties or filled with cream cheese and cut into finger sandwiches.

 *Lickety-Split Beer Rolls*

Wesson® No-Stick Cooking Spray
4 cups self-rising flour
¼ cup sugar
1 teaspoon salt
2 cups imported beer
½ cup Wesson® Canola Oil
1½ tablespoons caraway seeds

Preheat oven to 400°F. Spray muffin cups with Wesson Cooking Spray. In a large mixing bowl, combine flour, sugar and salt; blend well. Add beer and Wesson Oil; stir until dry ingredients are moistened. Fold in caraway seeds. Fill muffin cups to rim with batter; bake 30 to 35 minutes or until tops are golden brown. Cool for 5 minutes. Remove rolls from pan; cool on wire rack. Serve warm or cool.

Makes 1½ dozen rolls

These rolls are great served with Buttermilk Ranch Fried Chicken (pictured on the cover, recipe on page 58).

Sunday Morning Upside-Down Rolls

¼ cup warm water (105°F to 115°F)
1 envelope quick-rising yeast
¼ teaspoon sugar
1 cup scalded milk, slightly cooled
½ cup Wesson® Canola Oil
½ cup sugar
3 eggs, beaten
1½ teaspoons salt
4½ cups all-purpose flour
¾ cup (1½ sticks) butter, softened
2 cups packed brown sugar
1 cup maraschino cherries, chopped
1 (16-ounce) jar Knott's Berry Farm® Light Apricot
 Pineapple Preserves

Pour water into a large bowl. Sprinkle yeast, then *¼ teaspoon* sugar into water; stir well. Let stand 5 to 8 minutes or until mixture is slightly foamy. Meanwhile, in a small bowl, whisk milk, Wesson Oil, *½ cup* sugar, eggs and salt until well blended. Pour milk mixture into yeast mixture; blend well. Gradually add flour to mixture; mix until smooth. Knead dough in bowl (about 5 minutes) until smooth. Add more flour if dough is sticky. Cover with towel and let rise in a warm place for 30 minutes or until dough nearly doubles in size. Punch down dough once in the center; cover.

Meanwhile, in small bowl, cream together butter and brown sugar. Spoon (be careful not to pack) *2 teaspoons* of creamed sugar mixture into each of *24 muffin cups*. Sprinkle maraschino cherries over creamed sugar mixture; then add *2 teaspoons* Knott's preserves to each muffin cup. Tear small pillows of dough onto preserves, filling *each* muffin cup to the rim. Cover; let rise about 15 to 20 minutes. Preheat oven to 375°F. Bake for 12 to 15 minutes or until golden brown. Immediately invert rolls onto cookie sheet. ***Do not remove rolls from muffin cups.*** Allow a few minutes for preserves to drip down the sides. Lift muffin pans from rolls; cool 5 minutes. Remove muffins to wire rack. Serve warm.

Makes 2 dozen rolls

Salads, Sides & More

Your main dish deserves the best. Put your entrée in good company with these delicious soups, salads and family-pleasing side dishes.

Garden Vegetable Salad

⅔ cup red wine vinegar
½ cup Wesson® Vegetable Oil
1½ tablespoons fresh lemon juice
 1 teaspoon prepared horseradish
 1 teaspoon fresh minced garlic
½ teaspoon salt
¼ teaspoon coarsely ground black pepper
 2 cups peeled and thinly sliced carrots (¼ inch thick)
1½ cups thinly sliced zucchini (¼ inch thick)
 2 medium red onions, sliced and separated into rings
 1 cup cherry tomatoes, halved
½ cup julienned red bell pepper
⅓ cup crumbled blue cheese
 2 tablespoons chopped fresh basil
 2 tablespoons chopped fresh parsley
 1 tablespoon snipped chives

In a small bowl, combine *first* 7 ingredients, ending with pepper. Whisk vigorously until well blended; set aside. In a large bowl, combine carrots, zucchini, onions, tomatoes, bell peppers, *half* the blue cheese, basil and parsley. Pour dressing over vegetables; toss until well coated. Cover and refrigerate at least 2 hours, stirring occasionally. Stir once more before serving. Sprinkle *remaining* cheese and chives over salad.

Makes 8 servings

Garden Vegetable Salad

Nita Lou's Cream of Broccoli Soup

⅓ cup plus 1 tablespoon Wesson® Vegetable Oil
3 cups coarsely chopped broccoli florets and stems
1 cup diced carrots
1½ cups fresh chopped leeks
3 tablespoons all-purpose flour
1½ teaspoons minced fresh garlic
2 (12-ounce) cans evaporated milk
1½ cups homemade chicken stock or canned chicken broth
½ teaspoon garlic salt
¼ teaspoon ground nutmeg
⅛ teaspoon pepper
3 tablespoons chopped fresh parsley
Salt to taste

In a large saucepan, heat *3 tablespoons* Wesson Oil. Add broccoli and carrots; sauté until tender. Remove vegetables; set aside. Add *remaining* oil, leeks, flour and garlic; sauté until leeks are limp and flour is lightly browned, about 2 minutes, stirring constantly. Whisk in the evaporated milk and stock. Continue to cook, whisking constantly until the flour has dissolved and the mixture is smooth. ***Do not bring mixture to a boil.*** Reduce heat to LOW. Add cooked vegetables along with any juices, garlic salt, nutmeg and pepper. Simmer 5 minutes longer, being careful not to bring soup to a boil. Remove the pan from the heat; stir in parsley. Let soup stand 5 minutes before serving. Salt to taste.

Makes 6 servings

Country Corn Bread Dressing

Wesson® No-Stick Cooking Spray
1 (12-ounce) package seasoned corn bread stuffing
2½ cups dry bread crumbs
2 cups chopped celery
1 cup finely chopped onion
¼ cup (½ stick) butter
½ teaspoon poultry seasoning
¼ teaspoon pepper
2 (14½-ounce) cans chicken broth
¼ cup Wesson® Vegetable Oil

Preheat oven to 375°F. Spray a 13×9×2-inch baking dish with Wesson Cooking Spray; set aside. Combine stuffing mix and bread crumbs in a large bowl; set aside. In a medium saucepan, sauté celery and onion in butter until crisp-tender; blend in poultry seasoning and pepper. Add broth and Wesson Oil; bring to boil for 1 minute. Add to corn bread mixture; toss lightly to coat. Spoon corn bread mixture into baking dish; bake, uncovered, for 35 to 45 minutes or until golden brown.

Makes 10 to 12 servings

Red Cabbage Salad

1 cup Wesson® Best Blend Oil
1 cup cider vinegar
1 cup seasoned rice vinegar
⅔ cup sugar
1 tablespoon celery seed
2 teaspoons coarsely ground black pepper
2 teaspoons salt
1½ tablespoons chopped fresh dill weed *or* 1 teaspoon dried dill weed
2 to 2½ pounds red cabbage, shredded

Combine *all* ingredients *except* cabbage; mix until sugar is dissolved. Place cabbage in large bowl and pour dressing over cabbage; toss until completely coated. Cover and refrigerate at least 6 hours or up to 24 hours, tossing salad several times. Toss once before serving.

Makes 3 quarts salad

 # Blender Potato Soup

½ cup Wesson® Vegetable Oil
3 cups chopped celery
1½ cups chopped onions
1 teaspoon fresh minced garlic
1 quart chicken broth
3 cups peeled and diced russet potatoes
½ cup chopped fresh parsley
½ teaspoon salt
¼ teaspoon pepper
Shredded sharp Cheddar cheese

In a large saucepan, heat Wesson Oil. Add celery, onions and garlic; sauté until tender. Stir in *remaining* ingredients *except ⅓ cup* parsley and cheese; bring to a boil and reduce heat. Simmer, covered, for 20 minutes or until potatoes are tender. Pour *half* of mixture into blender; purée until smooth. Set aside. Pour *remaining* soup into blender; blend until coarsely chopped. Combine both mixtures. Ladle soup into bowls; garnish with *remaining* parsley and cheese.   *Makes 8 servings*

Little Reet's 24-Hour Marinated Salad

1 (15-ounce) can petite peas, drained
1 (14.5-ounce) can French-style green beans, drained
1 (11-ounce) can shoepeg white corn, drained
1 cup diced celery
1 cup diced red onion
1 medium red bell pepper, chopped
1 medium yellow bell pepper, chopped
1 medium green bell pepper, chopped
1 (2-ounce) jar pimientos, drained
¾ cup red wine vinegar
½ cup Wesson® Canola Oil
½ cup sugar

In a large bowl, combine *all* ingredients; mix well. Cover and refrigerate for 24 hours, stirring occasionally. Stir once before serving.
          Makes 8 to 10 servings

 *Georgia-Style Lemon Pilaf*

¼ **cup Wesson® Vegetable Oil**
½ **cup minced sweet onion**
½ **cup diced celery**
 1 **cup uncooked long-grain rice**
 1 **(14½-ounce) can chicken broth**
½ **cup water**
⅓ **cup dried currants**
 2 **tablespoons fresh lemon juice**
 2 **teaspoons grated fresh lemon peel**
¼ **cup sliced almonds, toasted**
 1 **tablespoon fresh chopped parsley**

In a large saucepan, heat Wesson Oil until hot. Add onion and celery;
sauté until crisp-tender. Add rice; continue sautéing an additional 3
minutes. Mix in *remaining* ingredients *except* almonds and parsley.
Bring mixture to a boil, stirring occasionally. Cover, reduce heat to
MEDIUM-LOW and cook until liquid is absorbed and rice is tender,
about 20 minutes. Mix in almonds and parsley; cover and let stand 5
minutes. Fluff with fork before serving.   *Makes 4 servings*

Pure
Wesson®

*For a special Sunday dinner, serve this dish with
Grilled Jumbo Shrimp (page 52) and
grilled vegetables.*

🕐 *Mrs. Farfsing's "One Dressing Fits All"*

1 cup Wesson® Vegetable Oil
⅔ cup red wine vinegar
1 teaspoon crushed fresh garlic
1 teaspoon Worcestershire sauce
1 teaspoon sugar
1 teaspoon salt
1 teaspoon dry mustard
1 teaspoon paprika
½ teaspoon coarsely ground pepper

Prepare this dressing early in the day. Pour *all* ingredients in a resealable glass jar or airtight plastic container; close tightly. Shake dressing vigorously until salt and sugar have dissolved and all ingredients have been well blended. Refrigerate until ready to serve; shake again vigorously just before serving.   *Makes 1⅔ cups*

This all-purpose dressing may be drizzled on a platter of steamed fresh vegetables or used to perk up potato and pasta salads.

Ben and Marcie's Collard Greens

2 bundles collard greens
2 bundles mustard greens
⅓ cup Wesson® Canola Oil
½ pound diced ham
½ cup chopped onion
½ teaspoon salt
¼ teaspoon pepper
¼ teaspoon garlic powder
1 (14½-ounce) can chicken broth
Gebhardt® Hot Pepper Sauce (optional)

Wash collard and mustard greens THOROUGHLY, making sure to wash
away any grit; drain. Coarsely chop or tear greens into medium-size
pieces. In a large Dutch oven or stockpot, heat Wesson Oil. Add ham
and onion; sauté until ham is brown and onion is tender. Stir in salt,
pepper and garlic powder. Add greens; sauté until greens start to wilt.
Add chicken broth; simmer for 20 minutes or until greens are tender,
adding more broth if necessary. Season with Gebhardt Hot Pepper
Sauce, if desired.   *Makes 6 to 8 servings*

Two-Day Sauerkraut Salad

1 (16-ounce) can sauerkraut, drained and chopped
¾ cup sugar
½ cup chopped red bell pepper
½ cup chopped green bell pepper
½ cup thinly sliced celery
½ cup Wesson® Best Blend Oil
½ cup apple cider vinegar
1 teaspoon dill seed

In a large serving bowl or resealable plastic bag, combine *all*
ingredients and toss well. Cover; refrigerate for **2 DAYS**, tossing 2 to 3
times a day. Drain liquid and serve cold.   *Makes 6 servings*

Miss Gayle's Southern Green Bean Salad

Dressing:
 ½ cup homemade chicken stock or canned chicken broth
 ⅓ cup Wesson® Vegetable Oil
 ⅓ cup white wine vinegar
 1 tablespoon Dijon mustard
 2 teaspoons salt
 ½ teaspoon dry mustard
 ¼ teaspoon coarsely ground black pepper
1½ teaspoons chopped fresh dill weed
1½ teaspoons chopped fresh parsley

Salad:
1¼ pounds freshly picked green beans, trimmed and cut
    into 2-inch pieces
 1 sprig fresh summer savory *or* ¼ teaspoon dried savory

Dressing: In a small bowl, combine *all* dressing ingredients *except* dill and parsley. Whisk together vigorously until well blended. Fold in dill and parsley; refrigerate.

Salad: In a large saucepan, bring 2 quarts water to a boil; add beans and savory. Blanch beans for 3 minutes, stirring occasionally. Carefully drain blanched green beans and immerse in ice water to stop cooking process; discard savory. Keep beans in water until completely cooled. Drain thoroughly and shake off excess water. If necessary, pat dry. Return green beans to bowl; top with dressing. Toss green beans to coat; cover and refrigerate at least 2 hours or overnight, tossing occasionally. Toss before serving. *Makes 6 servings*

This salad is the perfect partner for Southern Fried Chicken (page 46).

Vegetable Soup with Delicious Dumplings

Soup:
- 2 tablespoons Wesson® Vegetable Oil
- 1 cup diced onion
- ¾ cup sliced celery
- 7 cups homemade chicken broth *or* 4 (14½-ounce) cans chicken broth
- 2 (14.5-ounce) cans Hunt's® Stewed Tomatoes
- ½ teaspoon garlic powder
- ½ teaspoon salt
- ½ teaspoon fines herbs seasoning
- ⅛ teaspoon pepper
- 1 (16-ounce) bag frozen mixed vegetables
- 1 (15½-ounce) can Hunt's® Red Kidney Beans, drained
- ⅓ cup uncooked long-grain rice

Dumplings:
- 2 cups all-purpose flour
- 3 tablespoons baking powder
- 1 teaspoon salt
- ⅔ cup milk
- ⅓ cup Wesson® Vegetable Oil
- ½ tablespoon chopped fresh parsley

Soup: In a large Dutch oven, heat Wesson Oil. Add onion and celery; sauté until crisp-tender. Stir in *next 6* ingredients, ending with pepper; bring to a boil. Add vegetables, beans and rice. Reduce heat; cover and simmer 15 to 20 minutes or until rice is cooked and vegetables are tender.

Dumplings: Meanwhile, in a medium bowl, combine flour, baking powder and salt; blend well. Add milk, Wesson Oil and parsley; mix until batter forms a ball in the bowl. Drop dough by rounded tablespoons into simmering soup. Cook, covered, 10 minutes; remove lid and cook an additional 10 minutes.   *Makes 10 servings*

*Vegetable Soup with
Delicious Dumplings*

Farmers' Market Salad

Dressing:
  ½ cup chopped peperoncini
  ⅓ cup seasoned rice vinegar
  3 tablespoons country Dijon mustard
  2 tablespoons chopped fresh dill
1½ teaspoons sugar
1½ teaspoons garlic salt
1½ teaspoons fresh lemon juice
1½ teaspoons grated fresh lemon peel
  ½ teaspoon coarsely ground pepper
  ⅔ cup Wesson® Best Blend Oil

Salad:
  1 pound baby red potatoes, unpeeled
  1 pound baby asparagus
  1 pound mixed salad greens or spinach leaves, washed
     and drained
  1 basket cherry tomatoes, halved or baby teardrop yellow
     tomatoes
  1 large orange bell pepper, thinly sliced
  4 hard boiled eggs, quartered

Dressing: In blender or food processor, add *all dressing* ingredients *except* Wesson Oil. Pulse ingredients and slowly add Wesson Oil until dressing is partially smooth; refrigerate.

Salad: In a saucepan of water, cook potatoes until tender. Drain potatoes; immerse in ice water for 5 minutes to stop cooking process. Cool completely; drain well. In large pot of boiling water, cook asparagus until crisp-tender. Repeat cooling procedure with asparagus. In a large bowl, toss salad greens with ⅓ dressing. Evenly divide salad greens among 4 plates. Arrange potatoes, asparagus, tomatoes, bell pepper and eggs in sections over salad greens. Drizzle *half* the *remaining* dressing over arranged vegetables and eggs. Serve salad with *remaining* dressing, if desired.

Makes 4 servings

Green Bean Potato Salad

1½ **pounds slender green beans, ends trimmed and cut in half**
 6 **small red potatoes, cubed**
 1 **small red onion, thinly sliced lengthwise from stem to root**
¼ **cup Wesson® Canola Oil**
¼ **cup red wine vinegar**
¼ **cup seasoned rice vinegar**
 1 **tablespoon garlic salt**
1½ **teaspoons seasoned pepper**
 1 **teaspoon sugar**

In large pot of boiling water, cook green beans about 7 minutes until crisp-tender. Drain and immerse beans in ice water for 5 minutes to stop cooking process. Completely cool and drain well. In large pot of water, cook potatoes until tender. Repeat cooling procedure with potatoes. Place beans in a large serving bowl. Add potatoes and onion. In small bowl, whisk together Wesson Oil, vinegars, garlic salt, seasoned pepper and sugar. Pour dressing over vegetables; toss gently to coat. Cover and refrigerate 2 hours, tossing a few times during refrigeration. Remove salad from refrigerator a half hour before serving; toss just before serving.   *Makes 6 servings*

Garden Fresh Vegetable Bundles

 6 **large sheets of heavy aluminum foil**
   Wesson® No-Stick Cooking Spray
 2 **cups cubed potatoes (1-inch squares)**
 2 **cups sliced zucchini (2-inch slices)**
 1 **cup sliced carrots (¼-inch slices)**
 1 **cup diced red bell pepper (1-inch dice)**
 1 **cup diced green bell pepper (1-inch dice)**
 1 **cup broccoli florets (1-inch pieces)**
 1 **cup diced sweet onion (1-inch dice)**
 1 **large ear of corn, cut into 6 pieces**
¼ **cup Wesson® Vegetable Oil**
 3 **teaspoons Creole seasoning**
   Garlic salt

Preheat oven to 450°F. Spray *each* sheet of foil with Wesson Cooking Spray. In a large bowl, combine *next 8* ingredients, ending with corn. Toss with Wesson Oil. Evenly divide vegetable mixture among prepared sheets of foil. Sprinkle *½ teaspoon* Creole seasoning on *each* vegetable packet. Sprinkle with desired amount of garlic salt. Bring sides of foil to center and fold over to seal. Fold ends to center, creating a tight bundle. Repeat with *remaining* packets. Place bundles on cookie sheet; bake for 30 minutes or until vegetables are tender.   *Makes 6 servings*

This recipe also works great on the grill!

Creamy Tomato & Herb Dressing

1 (14.5-ounce) can Hunt's® Choice-Cut Tomatoes with
    Roasted Garlic, undrained
¼ cup cider vinegar
¼ cup mayonnaise
¼ cup chopped fresh parsley
2 tablespoons chopped fresh basil
2 tablespoons spicy brown mustard
1 teaspoon sugar
1 teaspoon minced fresh garlic
½ cup Wesson® Vegetable Oil
    Salt and pepper to taste

Purée *all* ingredients *except* Wesson Oil, salt and pepper in food processor about 20 seconds. Pulse food processor on and off, about 10 seconds, while gradually adding oil. Salt and pepper to taste. Cover; refrigerate 1 hour or up to 24 hours. Shake well before serving.

Makes 3 cups

Potato and Egg Pie

1 (20-ounce) package frozen O'Brien hash brown potatoes,
     thawed
⅓ cup Wesson® Vegetable Oil
1½ tablespoons chopped fresh parsley
¾ cup shredded pepper-jack cheese
¾ cup shredded Swiss cheese
1 (12-ounce) package bulk breakfast sausage, cooked,
     crumbled and drained
1 (4-ounce) can sliced mushrooms, drained
½ cup milk
4 eggs, beaten
1 teaspoon garlic salt
¼ teaspoon pepper
4 to 6 thin tomato slices

Preheat oven to 425°F. In a medium bowl, combine potatoes and
Wesson Oil; blend to coat. Press mixture into a 10-inch pie dish. Bake
for 30 minutes or until golden brown; remove from oven. Reduce oven
temperature to 350°F. Meanwhile, in a large bowl, combine *1 tablespoon*
parsley and *remaining* ingredients *except* tomato slices; blend well.
Pour into potato crust. Bake for 25 minutes or until eggs are set. Place
tomato slices over pie and top with *remaining* parsley. Bake 5 to 7
minutes longer.   *Makes 6 servings*

*For a special family brunch, serve this hearty
dish with Sunday Morning Upside-Down Rolls
(page 20) and a fresh fruit salad.*

Fresh & Fancy Cucumber Salad

2 medium cucumbers, unpeeled (about 1½ to 1¾ pound)
⅔ cup seasoned rice vinegar
⅓ cup Wesson® Canola Oil
1½ tablespoons chopped fresh dill *or* 1 teaspoon dried dill weed
½ teaspoon salt
½ teaspoon sugar
Pinch pepper
1½ cups red onion wedges (⅛ inch thick)

Slightly piercing cucumbers, run fork tines down length of cucumbers on *all* sides; thinly slice. In a medium bowl, combine vinegar, Wesson Oil, dill, salt, sugar and pepper; mix until sugar is dissolved. Toss in cucumbers and onions; mix until vegetables are well coated with dressing. Refrigerate 15 minutes. Toss salad before serving. Serve with slotted spoon.   *Makes 4 to 6 servings*

Sassy French Dressing

1 (8-ounce) can Hunt's® Tomato Sauce
½ cup Wesson® Vegetable Oil
⅓ cup rice vinegar
1 tablespoon light brown sugar
½ teaspoon salt
¼ teaspoon dry mustard
⅛ teaspoon garlic powder

Combine *all* ingredients in a cruet or jar; shake well. Refrigerate for at least 30 minutes. Shake well before serving.   *Makes 2 cups*

Summer Salad

Maudice Livingston
Charlotte, North Carolina
1996 Wesson Cookers' Club Recipe Contest Winner

Salad:
2 cups *each:* broccoli florets, diced spring onions, julienne-cut bell peppers, julienne-cut carrots, cubed tomatoes, diagonally cut celery, halved snow peas

Dressing:
⅓ cup Wesson® Canola Oil
⅓ cup LaChoy® Lite Soy Sauce
⅓ cup Worcestershire sauce
1 tablespoon blackened seasoning
1 tablespoon seasoned salt
1 tablespoon garlic salt
2 teaspoons minced fresh garlic

Salad: In a large bowl, combine *all* salad ingredients.

Dressing: Add *all* dressing ingredients to salad mixture. Toss salad well to coat. Cover and refrigerate at least 20 minutes. Toss before serving.

Makes 6 to 8 servings

Maudice also recommends serving this dish hot as a stir-fry. Simply heat up your skillet and use this flavorful dressing instead of oil.

Blue Cheese and Bacon Griddle Cakes

¾ cup cornmeal
¾ cup all-purpose flour
1 teaspoon baking powder
¼ teaspoon baking soda
¼ teaspoon salt
1½ cups buttermilk
3 large eggs, separated
⅓ cup Wesson® Vegetable Oil
1 (6-ounce) package crumbled blue cheese
½ cup chopped green onions
½ cup crumbled bacon
½ teaspoon salt
½ teaspoon garlic powder
⅛ teaspoon pepper
Toppings: sour cream, cheese sauce, guacamole or salsa

In a large bowl, mix the *first 5* ingredients, ending with salt. In another bowl, whisk together buttermilk, egg yolks and *1½ tablespoons* Wesson Oil. Add buttermilk mixture to flour mixture; stir until well blended. Stir in blue cheese and *next 5* ingredients, ending with pepper. In a medium bowl, beat egg whites to form stiff peaks. Fold whites into batter in two additions. In large skillet, heat *1 tablespoon* Wesson Oil. Working in batches, pour *¼ cup* batter into skillet. Cook, turning once, until cakes are puffy and golden brown. Add more Wesson Oil for *each* batch to avoid sticking. Serve hot with your favorite topping.

Makes 18 (4-inch) griddle cakes

Main Dishes

When you are cooking one of these dishes, you won't have to call them to the table twice. These are the recipes your family will be asking for again and again.

Southern Fried Chicken

2½ to 3 pounds frying chicken pieces
    Wesson® Vegetable Oil
2 cups self-rising flour
2 teaspoons salt
1 teaspoon pepper
1 teaspoon paprika
1 teaspoon onion powder
½ teaspoon ground sage
¼ teaspoon garlic powder
2 eggs beaten with 2 tablespoons water

Rinse chicken and pat dry; set aside. Fill a large deep-fry pot or electric skillet to no more than half its depth with Wesson Oil. Heat oil to 325°F to 350°F. In bag, combine flour and seasonings. Shake chicken, one piece at a time, in flour mixture until coated. Dip in egg mixture, then shake again in flour mixture until completely coated. Fry chicken, a few pieces at a time, skin side down, for 10 to 14 minutes. Turn and fry chicken 10 minutes, covered, then 3 to 5 minutes, uncovered, or until chicken is tender and juices run clear. Drain on paper towels. Let stand 7 minutes before serving. *Makes 4 to 6 servings*

Southern Fried Chicken

 *Cheatin' Jambalaya*

⅓ cup **Wesson® Vegetable Oil**
½ cup **chopped onion**
½ cup **sliced celery**
½ cup **chopped bell pepper**
½ cup **sliced okra (½-inch slices)**
½ teaspoon **minced fresh garlic**
1 pound **kielbasa sausage, cut into ½-inch pieces**
1 (15-ounce) can **Hunt's® Tomato Sauce**
¼ cup **white wine or homemade chicken stock**
1 teaspoon **Worcestershire sauce**
⅛ teaspoon **crushed red pepper**
5 drops **Gebhardt® Hot Pepper Sauce (optional)**
    Hot cooked brown rice

In a large pot or deep skillet, heat Wesson Oil. Add onion, celery, bell pepper, okra and garlic; sauté until tender. Stir in *remaining* ingredients *except* rice. Simmer, covered, 15 minutes, stirring occasionally. Serve over rice.

Makes 4 servings

Betty Jo's Sausage and Cheese Grits

    Wesson® No-Stick Cooking Spray
1 pound **mild or hot cooked sausage, crumbled and drained**
1½ cups **grits**
2½ cups **shredded Cheddar cheese**
3 tablespoons **Wesson® Vegetable Oil**
1½ cups **milk**
3 **eggs, slightly beaten**

Preheat oven to 350°F. Lightly spray a 13×9×2-inch baking dish with Wesson Cooking Spray. Evenly spread crumbled sausage on bottom of dish; set aside. Bring 4½ cups water to a boil in a large saucepan. Stir in grits and lower heat. Cook 5 minutes until thickened, stirring occasionally. Add cheese and Wesson Oil; stir until cheese has melted. Stir in milk and eggs; blend well. Evenly spoon mixture over sausage; bake, uncovered, 1 hour or until grits have set.

Makes 6 to 8 servings

Geneva's Fried Chicken

Geneva Burress
Memphis, Tennessee
1996 Wesson Cookers' Club Recipe Contest Winner

Wesson® Vegetable Oil
10 chicken legs
6 bone-in chicken breasts
Seasoned salt
Garlic powder
Black pepper
Self-rising flour (about 1½ to 2 cups)

Fill a large deep-fryer or skillet to half its depth with Wesson Oil. Heat to 420°F. Rinse chicken and pat dry. Generously sprinkle seasoned salt, garlic powder and black pepper on both sides of chicken pieces. Dredge chicken in flour; gently shake off excess flour. Fry chicken 10 to 15 minutes or until juices run clear; drain on paper towels. Let chicken stand for 7 minutes before serving.   *Makes 4 to 6 servings*

Geneva serves her fried chicken with homemade spicy French fries cooked in the same oil as the chicken and sprinkled with seasoned salt.

"All the Fixings" Turkey Pot Roast

1 large oven bag
1 (2- to 2½-pound) turkey breast half
⅓ cup Wesson® Canola Oil
Seasoned salt
Seasoned pepper
1 large sweet onion, sliced ¼ inch thick
8 carrots, peeled and cut in half
4 small russet potatoes, sliced in half lengthwise
Garlic salt

Preheat oven to 350°F. Place oven bag in a 13×9×2-inch baking dish. Loosen and fold back skin from meat of turkey breast but do not totally detach. Generously brush breast with Wesson Oil and place in oven bag. Sprinkle a generous amount of seasoned salt and seasoned pepper on meat. Top meat with 4 to 5 slices of onion. Brush onions with oil; then cover onions with skin. Generously brush entire breast with oil and sprinkle with seasoned salt and pepper. Brush carrots, potatoes and *remaining* onion slices with oil; sprinkle with garlic salt and seasoned pepper. Place vegetables around turkey breast and close bag; cut four ½-inch slits through top of bag. Bake for 1½ to 2 hours or until turkey juices run clear.   *Makes 4 to 6 servings*

Complete this meal with
Lickety-Split Beer Rolls (page 19).

 *Fish and Suds*

   1 cup self-rising flour
   1 cup beer
   1 egg
   2 tablespoons malt vinegar
1½ teaspoons garlic salt
   1 teaspoon cayenne pepper
 ½ teaspoon dry mustard
   1 pound white fish fillets
     Wesson® Vegetable Oil

In a medium bowl, whisk together flour, beer, egg, malt vinegar, garlic salt, pepper and dry mustard; blend well. Let batter stand 20 minutes. Meanwhile, rinse fish and pat dry; place on paper towels. Fill a large deep-fry skillet to no more than half its depth with Wesson Oil. Heat oil to 325°F. Dip fish, one piece at a time, in batter; coat well. Fry fish 2 to 3 minutes, turning once. (Fish should brown immediately.) Drain on paper towels; serve hot.   *Makes 4 servings*

Grilled Jumbo Shrimp

24 raw jumbo shrimp, shelled and deveined
 1 cup Wesson® Canola Oil
½ cup minced fresh onion
 2 teaspoons dried oregano
 1 teaspoon salt
 1 teaspoon crushed fresh garlic
½ teaspoon dried sweet basil
½ teaspoon dried thyme
 3 tablespoons fresh lemon juice
 6 long bamboo skewers, soaked in water for 20 minutes

Rinse shrimp and pat dry; set aside. In a large bowl, whisk together
Wesson Oil and *next 6* ingredients, ending with thyme. Reserve *⅓ cup*
marinade; set aside. Toss shrimp in marinade; cover and refrigerate
3 hours, tossing occasionally. Stir in lemon juice; let stand at room
temperature for 30 minutes. Meanwhile, preheat grill or broiler. Drain
shrimp; discard marinade. Thread *4 shrimp* per skewer. Grill shrimp,
4 inches over hot coals, 3 minutes per side or until pink, basting with
remaining ⅓ cup marinade.   *Makes 6 servings*

 ## *Fresh & Easy Spaghetti Sauce*

⅓ cup Wesson® Best Blend Oil
½ pound sliced fresh mushrooms
 1 cup chopped onions
¼ cup chopped fresh parsley
¼ cup chopped fresh basil, lightly packed
 1 tablespoon fresh minced garlic
 3 (14.5-ounce) cans Hunt's® Whole Tomatoes, undrained
      and crushed
 1 (8-ounce) can Hunt's® Tomato Sauce
 1 (6-ounce) can Hunt's® Tomato Paste
⅛ teaspoon pepper

In a Dutch oven, heat Wesson Oil. Add mushrooms, onions, parsley, basil
and garlic; sauté until onions are tender. Stir in *remaining* ingredients.
Simmer, covered, 30 minutes or until thickened, stirring often. Serve
over hot cooked spaghetti.   *Makes 4 servings*

Grilled Jumbo Shrimp

Vegetable Cobbler

Cobbler:

Wesson® No-Stick Cooking Spray
1 medium butternut squash, peeled and cut into
    1½-inch pieces
3 medium red potatoes, unpeeled and cut into 1½-inch
    pieces
3 medium parsnips, peeled and cut into 1-inch pieces
1 medium red onion, cut into 6 wedges
¼ cup Wesson® Vegetable Oil
1 tablespoon chopped fresh dill weed
1 teaspoon salt
¾ cup homemade chicken stock or canned chicken broth
½ cup milk
1 (15-ounce) can pears, cut into 1-inch pieces, juice
    reserved
1 tablespoon cornstarch
4 cups broccoli florets
1 teaspoon grated fresh lemon peel

Topping:

1¾ cups all-purpose baking mix
¾ cup shredded Cheddar cheese
½ cup cornmeal
1 tablespoon chopped fresh dill weed
¾ teaspoon coarsely ground pepper
¾ cup milk

Cobbler: Preheat oven to 400°F. Spray a 13×9×2-inch baking dish with Wesson Cooking Spray. In prepared baking dish, toss *all* vegetables *except* broccoli with Wesson Oil, dill and salt to coat. Bake, covered, 40 to 45 minutes. Meanwhile, in saucepan, combine broth, milk, reserved pear juice and cornstarch; blend well. Bring to a boil. Add broccoli and lemon peel and cook until slightly thick; set aside.

Topping: In a small bowl, combine *all* topping ingredients; mix with fork until well blended.

Stir vegetables in baking dish. Add chopped pears; gently mix. Pour broccoli sauce evenly over vegetables. Drop 12 heaping spoonfuls of topping evenly over vegetables. Bake, uncovered, for 15 minutes or until topping is golden.   *Makes 8 servings*

Citrus Grove Marinated Salmon

4 salmon fillets or steaks
⅓ cup lemonade concentrate, thawed
¼ cup Wesson® Vegetable Oil
¼ cup orange juice concentrate, thawed
½ tablespoon fresh dill weed *or* ½ teaspoon dried dill weed
   Wesson® No-Stick Cooking Spray

Rinse salmon and pat dry; set aside. In a small bowl, combine *remaining* ingredients *except* Wesson Cooking Spray. Place salmon in a large resealable plastic food storage bag; pour ¾ *marinade* over fish; set *remaining* marinade aside. Seal bag and gently turn to coat; refrigerate 2 hours, turning several times during marinating. Preheat broiler. Line a jelly-roll pan with foil; spray with Wesson Cooking Spray. Place fish in pan; discard used marinade. Broil fish until it flakes easily with a fork, basting frequently with *remaining* ¼ marinade and once before serving.   *Makes 4 servings*

Chicken in the Hay

⅓ cup Wesson® Best Blend Oil
2 cups frozen shredded hash brown potatoes, thawed
¾ cup sliced green onions
1½ cups seasoned croutons
6 large eggs, beaten
¾ cup diced ham
⅔ cup shredded Cheddar cheese
⅛ to ¼ teaspoon coarsely ground pepper (optional)
   Salt to taste
   Shredded Cheddar cheese for garnish

In a large skillet, heat Wesson Oil. Add hash browns and green onions; fry until potatoes are dark golden brown, stirring occasionally. If potatoes become dry, add more oil. Add *remaining* ingredients *except* salt and cheese for garnish; blend well. Cook egg mixture until eggs are set. Salt to taste and garnish with additional cheese.   *Makes 6 servings*

Buttermilk Ranch Fried Chicken

2½ to 3 pounds frying chicken pieces
   Wesson® Vegetable Oil
2¼ cups all-purpose flour
1¼ tablespoons dried dill weed
1½ teaspoons salt
 ¾ teaspoon pepper
2½ cups buttermilk

Rinse chicken and pat dry; set aside. Fill a large deep-fry pot or electric skillet to no more than half its depth with Wesson Oil. Heat oil to 325°F to 350°F. In a medium bowl, combine flour, dill, salt and pepper. Fill another bowl with buttermilk. Place chicken, one piece at a time, in buttermilk; shake off excess liquid. Coat lightly in flour mixture; shake off excess flour. Dip once again in buttermilk and flour mixture. Fry chicken, a few pieces at a time, skin side down, for 10 to 14 minutes. Turn chicken and fry 12 to 15 minutes longer or until juices run clear; drain on paper towels. Let stand 7 minutes before serving.

Makes 4 to 6 servings

To reduce frying time by 7 to 9 minutes per side, simply cook unbreaded chicken in boiling water for 15 minutes; remove and cool completely before proceeding with recipe.

Pork Ribs with Apricot BBQ Sauce

2 (15-ounce) cans Hunt's® Ready Tomato Sauces Chunky
   Salsa
1 (16-ounce) jar Knott's Berry Farm® Apricot Preserves
½ cup finely diced onion
¼ cup Wesson® Vegetable Oil
1 teaspoon garlic salt
1 teaspoon dry mustard
3 pounds baby back ribs

Combine *all* ingredients *except* ribs; mix well. Place ribs in a large resealable plastic bag. Pour in *half* the barbecue sauce; set aside *remaining* sauce. Refrigerate ribs at least 1 hour. Rotate ribs in sauce 2 to 3 times while marinating. Remove from refrigerator a half hour before cooking. Preheat oven to 350°F. Place ribs on foil-lined baking pan; discard used sauce. Cover and bake 30 minutes. Meanwhile, preheat the grill. Place ribs on hot grill; baste ribs with ¾ *remaining* sauce. Grill ribs until meat is cooked through, about 30 minutes. Brush with *remaining* sauce before serving. *Makes 6 servings*

Biscuits 'n Gravy

Biscuits:
    Wesson® No-Stick Cooking Spray
  2 cups self-rising flour
  2 teaspoons sugar
1½ teaspoons baking powder
  ¾ cup buttermilk
  ¼ cup Wesson® Vegetable Oil

Gravy:
  1 pound bulk pork sausage
  ¼ cup all-purpose flour
  2 cups milk
  ¼ teaspoon salt
  ¼ teaspoon pepper

Biscuits: Preheat oven to 450°F. Lightly spray a baking sheet with Wesson Cooking Spray. In a large bowl, combine flour, sugar and baking powder; blend well. In a small bowl, whisk together buttermilk and Wesson Oil; add to dry ingredients and mix until dough is moist but not sticky. On a lightly floured surface, knead dough lightly 4 or 5 times. Roll dough to a ¾-inch thickness; cut with a 4-inch biscuit cutter. Knead any scraps together and repeat cutting method. Place biscuits on baking sheet and bake 10 to 15 minutes or until lightly browned. Keep warm.

Gravy: Meanwhile, in a large skillet, cook and crumble sausage until brown. Reserve ¼ cup of drippings in skillet; drain sausage well. Set aside. Add flour to drippings in skillet; stir until smooth. Cook over medium heat for 2 to 3 minutes or until dark brown, stirring constantly. Gradually add milk, stirring constantly until smooth and thickened. (Use more milk if necessary to achieve desired consistency.) Stir in salt, pepper and sausage; heat through. Serve over hot split biscuits.

Makes 6 servings (2 biscuits each)

Firehouse Marinated Steak

¼ cup Wesson® Best Blend or Vegetable Oil
 6 dried pasilla or ancho chilies, seeded and cut into strips
 1 cup coarsely chopped onion
1½ teaspoons chopped fresh garlic
 ½ cup beef broth
 2 tablespoons fresh lime juice
 2 teaspoons cumin seed
1½ teaspoons salt
 1 teaspoon brown sugar
 4 New York steaks *or* 1 (2-pound) flank steak, tenderized
    lightly with meat mallet
 2 limes

In a medium skillet, heat Wesson Oil over medium-low heat. Add
chilies, onion and garlic; sauté until onion is tender. *Do not drain.* Pour
onion mixture into blender. Add *remaining* ingredients *except* steaks
and limes; blend until smooth. If marinade is too thick, add additional
beef broth. Place steaks in large resealable plastic food storage bag. Pour
half the marinade over steaks; set aside *remaining* marinade. Seal bag
and turn to coat. Marinate in refrigerator for 30 minutes. Bring steaks to
room temperature. Over hot coals, grill steaks while basting with ¾ of
reserved marinade. Grill to desired doneness. Before serving, brush beef
with *remaining* ¼ marinade and generously squeeze fresh lime juice
over steaks.   *Makes 4 servings*

*This spicy marinade can be made up to 3 days
ahead of time; the flavors improve with age.*

Harvest Pork Roast

¼ cup Wesson® Best Blend Oil
2½ cups cubed onions (½-inch dice)
1½ teaspoons fresh minced garlic
¾ cup honey
¼ cup Dijon mustard
1½ teaspoons coarsely ground pepper
     Wesson® No-Stick Cooking Spray
3½ to 4 pounds boned pork shoulder roast, trimmed
4 large Red Delicious apples, quartered and cored
3 acorn squash, sliced horizontally 1½ inch thick
1 cup fresh cranberries

Preheat oven to 350°F. In a large skillet, heat Wesson Oil. Add onions and garlic; sauté until onions are crisp-tender. Remove from heat. Add honey, mustard and pepper to onions and garlic in skillet; mix well. Spray a large roasting pan with Wesson Cooking Spray. Place pork roast in the center of roasting pan. Pour onion mixture evenly over roast. Bake, covered, for 1½ hours, basting often with pan juices. Arrange apples and squash around roast. Baste roast, apples and squash several times with pan juices; cover. Bake an additional hour, basting occasionally, or until apples and squash are tender. Sprinkle cranberries evenly over dish. Bake, uncovered, for 10 minutes.

Makes 4 to 6 servings

*If fresh cranberries are not available, use
⅔ cup dried cranberries.*

Pan-Fried Stuffed Chicken

⅓ **cup diced sweet onion**
 2 **tablespoons chopped fresh parsley**
 2 **tablespoons grated Parmesan cheese**
½ **teaspoon salt**
¼ **teaspoon pepper**
¼ **teaspoon garlic powder**
¼ **teaspoon paprika**
 4 **(1-ounce) slices Swiss cheese**
 4 **boneless, skinless chicken breasts halves, pounded to**
     ⅛-**inch thickness**
½ **cup seasoned dry bread crumbs**
 2 **tablespoons grated Parmesan cheese**
⅓ **cup all-purpose flour**
 2 **eggs, lightly beaten**
½ **cup Wesson® Vegetable Oil**

In a small bowl, combine *first* 7 ingredients, ending with paprika; mix well and set aside. Place 1 slice of cheese in center of *each* chicken breast. Top with ¼ onion mixture. Starting with long edge, tightly roll breast, folding in ends to seal. Secure with toothpicks. In a small bowl, combine bread crumbs and 2 tablespoons Parmesan cheese. Dredge *each* breast in flour. Dip *each* breast in egg and then roll in bread crumbs. In a large skillet, heat Wesson Oil over medium heat. Fry chicken, starting with seam side down, rotating 7 to 10 minutes to avoid overbrowning. Fry 20 to 30 minutes or until golden brown and juices run clear. Drain on paper towels.   *Makes 4 servings*

Impress everyone even when you're busy.
Chicken can be wrapped individually and
frozen up to 2 months. Simply defrost and
proceed with the recipe.

Pan-Fried Stuffed Chicken

Stick-to-Your-Ribs Hearty Beef Stew

1½ **pounds lean beef stew meat, cut into bite-size pieces**
¼ **cup all-purpose flour**
½ **teaspoon seasoned salt**
⅓ **cup Wesson® Vegetable Oil**
2 **medium onions, cut into 1-inch pieces**
1 **(14½-ounce) can beef broth**
1 **(8-ounce) can Hunt's® Tomato Sauce**
4 **medium potatoes, peeled and cubed**
5 **stalks celery, cut into 1-inch pieces**
6 **carrots, peeled and cut into 1-inch pieces**
1½ **teaspoons salt**
½ **teaspoon Italian seasoning**
½ **teaspoon pepper**
1 **tablespoon cornstarch plus 2 tablespoons water**

In a bag, toss beef with flour and seasoned salt until well coated. In a large Dutch oven, in hot Wesson Oil, brown beef with onions until tender. Add *remaining* ingredients *except* cornstarch mixture; stir until well blended. Bring to a boil; reduce heat and simmer, covered, for 1 hour 15 minutes or until beef is tender. Stir cornstarch mixture; whisk into stew. Continue to cook an additional 10 minutes, stirring occasionally.   *Makes 6 to 8 servings*

For a fancier stew, reduce beef broth by ½ cup and add ½ cup red wine.

Fried Trout with Dill Sauce

Fish:
   4 small fresh trout, trimmed and cleaned
      Seasoned salt
   ½ cup all-purpose flour
   1 cup Wesson® Vegetable Oil

Sauce:
1½ tablespoons butter
   1 (12-ounce) package sliced mushrooms
   ¾ cup sliced green onions
1½ tablespoons all-purpose flour
   ¾ cup homemade chicken stock or canned chicken broth
   ¾ cup white wine
   3 tablespoons minced fresh dill *or* ½ tablespoon dried dill
      weed
   ½ tablespoon fresh lemon juice
   ¾ cup sour cream
1½ teaspoons garlic salt
   ¼ teaspoon pepper

   4 cups hot cooked rice

Fish: Rinse trout and pat dry. Sprinkle both sides with seasoned salt.
Dredge fish in flour. In a large skillet, heat Wesson Oil to 325°F. Fry fish
on both sides until fish flakes easily with fork; remove from skillet and
set aside.

Sauce: Meanwhile, melt butter in saucepan. Add mushrooms and
onions; sauté until mushrooms are browned and tender. Stir in flour.
Whisk in broth, wine, dill and lemon juice; stir until sauce boils and
thickens. Remove sauce from heat. Whisk in sour cream, garlic salt and
pepper; stir until smooth. Return sauce to LOW heat, stirring constantly
until heated through.

Spoon rice onto large serving platter; carefully place trout on top of
rice. Spoon sauce over fish.   *Makes 4 servings*

68

Other Fried Favorites

Nothing gives food more crunch and more mouthwatering flavor than frying, so heat up the oil for one of these tried and true recipes.

Old-Fashioned Onion Rings

½ cup buttermilk
½ cup prepared Ranch dressing
2 large onions, sliced ½-inch thick and separated into
    rings
    Wesson® Vegetable or Canola Oil
2 cups self-rising flour
2 teaspoons garlic salt
2 teaspoons lemon pepper
½ teaspoon cayenne pepper
2 eggs, slightly beaten with 2 tablespoons water

In a large bowl, combine buttermilk and Ranch dressing; blend well. Add onions and toss until well coated. Cover; refrigerate at least 1 hour or overnight. Fill a large deep-fry pot or electric skillet to no more than half its depth with Wesson Oil. Heat oil between 325°F to 350°F. In a large bowl, combine flour, garlic salt, lemon pepper and cayenne pepper; blend well. Working in small batches, place onion rings in flour mixture; coat well. Remove; dip into egg mixture. Return rings to flour mixture; coat well. Lightly shake off excess flour; fry until golden brown. Drain on paper towels. Sprinkle with additional garlic salt, if desired. *Makes 4 servings*

Old-Fashioned Onion Rings

Spicy Fried Chicken Wings

Maudice Livingston
Charlotte, North Carolina
1996 Wesson Cookers' Club Recipe Contest Winner

⅓ cup LaChoy® Lite Soy Sauce
⅓ cup Worcestershire sauce
2 tablespoons blackened seasoning
2 tablespoons garlic salt
2 tablespoons onion salt
2 tablespoons seasoned salt
2 tablespoons packed brown sugar
10 chicken wings
    Wesson® Vegetable Oil

In a large resealable plastic food storage bag, combine *first* 7 ingredients, ending with brown sugar. Seal tightly; shake vigorously until well blended and sugar is dissolved. Place chicken in bag; reseal bag. Toss chicken in marinade to coat. Refrigerate at least 1 hour or up to 24 hours, turning chicken several times. Fill a deep-fry pot or electric skillet to no more than half its depth with Wesson Oil. Heat oil to 325°F. Working in batches, fry wings for 7 minutes or until juices run clear; drain on paper towels.

Makes 10 wings

After you've finished frying the Spicy Fried Chicken Wings, leave the fryer on and make some Old-Fashioned Onion Rings (page 68) or Vala's Finest Corn Fritters (page 78).

Homemade Potato Chips

Sharon R. Robertson
Belmont, North Carolina
1996 Wesson Cookers' Club Recipe Contest Winner

    Wesson® Vegetable Oil
2 large russet potatoes, unpeeled
    Salt

Fill a large deep-fry pot or electric skillet to no more than half its depth with Wesson Oil. Heat oil to 350°F. Meanwhile, wash and scrub potatoes. Fill a large bowl with cold water three-fourths full. Slice potatoes crosswise into extremely thin pieces (about ¹⁄₁₆ inch); immerse slices in water. Working in small batches, remove potatoes with a slotted spoon; place on paper towels to dry. Fry 2 to 3 minutes or until golden brown and crispy. Remove from oil; drain on paper towels. Immediately salt to taste.   *Makes 4 to 6 servings*

For perfectly golden brown, crispy chips, make sure the oil temperature remains at 350°F.

Fried Green Tomatoes

½ **pound sliced bacon**
1 **cup cornmeal**
1 **cup all-purpose flour**
2 **teaspoons salt**
½ **teaspoon black pepper**
½ **teaspoon cayenne pepper**
3 **eggs, slightly beaten**
2 **cups Wesson® Corn Oil**
6 to 8 **green tomatoes, sliced ¼ to ½ inch thick**

In a large skillet, fry bacon until crisp; drain on paper towels. Crumble bacon; set aside. Reserve bacon drippings in the skillet. In a medium bowl, combine cornmeal, flour, salt and peppers; mix well. In a small bowl, combine egg and *half* the crumbled bacon; mix well. Heat Wesson Oil over medium heat in same skillet with bacon drippings. Sprinkle tomatoes lightly with salt; dip in egg mixture, making sure to press bacon pieces onto tomatoes. Place tomatoes in cornmeal mixture; gently press mixture onto both sides of tomatoes. Fry until light golden brown, turning once. Drain on paper towels. Sprinkle with *remaining* bacon and serve.   *Makes 20 to 25 fried tomatoes*

Hot Hush Puppies

Cindy Lynn
Charlotte, North Carolina
1996 Wesson Cookers' Club Recipe Contest Winner

Wesson® Vegetable Oil
1¾ cups cornmeal
½ cup all-purpose flour
1 teaspoon sugar
¾ teaspoon baking soda
½ teaspoon salt
½ teaspoon garlic salt
½ cup diced onion
½ to 1 (4-ounce) can diced jalapeño peppers
1 cup buttermilk
1 egg, beaten

Fill a large deep-fry pot or electric skillet to half its depth with Wesson Oil. Heat oil to 400°F. Meanwhile, in a large bowl, sift together cornmeal, flour, sugar, baking soda, salt and garlic salt; blend well. Add onion and jalapeño peppers; stir until well blended. In small bowl, combine buttermilk and egg; add to dry ingredients. Stir until batter is moist and *all* ingredients are combined. Working in small batches, carefully drop batter by heaping tablespoons into hot oil. Fry until golden brown, turning once during frying. Remove and drain on paper towels. Serve with your favorite salsa or dipping sauce.   *Makes 36 hush puppies*

Cindy keeps the ingredients for Hot Hush Puppies on hand to make on the spur of the moment when her teenaged daughter brings friends over after school.

Quick & Easy Salmon Cakes
Carla Kellogg
Memphis, Tennessee
1996 Wesson Cookers' Club Recipe Contest Winner

  1 (12-ounce) can pink salmon, undrained
  ⅓ **cup diced onion**
  1 egg, lightly beaten
  ½ **cup all-purpose flour**
1½ **teaspoons baking powder**
1½ **cups Wesson® Vegetable Oil**

Thoroughly drain salmon; reserve 2 tablespoons juice. In a medium bowl, flake salmon with a fork. Add reserved salmon juice, onion and egg; blend well. In a small bowl, combine flour and baking powder; gradually add to salmon mixture. Blend well. Evenly divide mixture into *6 balls.* Pat balls into patties. In a large skillet, heat Wesson Oil to 350°F. Fry patties on *each* side until golden brown. Remove from oil; drain on paper towels. Serve warm.   *Makes 6 patties*

Looking for a tasty appetizer to serve at your next party? Form the salmon cake mixture into 20 to 24 small balls and deep-fry for 2 to 3 minutes. Serve with a squeeze of lemon juice or tartar sauce.

Spicy Fried Potatoes & Seasoned Fried Fish

Jo Ann Anthony
Harahan, Louisiana
1996 Wesson Cookers' Club Recipe Contest Winner

Spicy Fried Potatoes:
  6 russet potatoes, washed and peeled
  1 (8-ounce) bottle crawfish and seafood boil liquid
     concentrate
1½ tablespoons salt
    Wesson® Vegetable Oil

Seasoned Fried Fish:
  2 pounds catfish fillets, cut into 1½- to 2-inch-wide strips
    Salt
1½ (3-ounce) boxes seasoned fish fry dry mix
    Wesson® Vegetable Oil

Spicy Fried Potatoes: Thinly slice potatoes smaller than French fries. Place slices in a bowl of water to prevent browning. In another bowl, pour ⅔ *cup* liquid concentrate, ½ cup warm water and salt; stir until salt is dissolved. Drain water from potatoes; place potatoes in seasoned water and toss to coat. Cover and refrigerate potatoes for 2 hours, stirring occasionally. Drain in colander for 20 minutes before frying. Meanwhile, fill 2 deep-fry pots or electric skillets to half their depth with Wesson Oil. Heat oil to 350°F.

Seasoned Fried Fish: Rinse fish and pat dry; sprinkle with salt. Dredge fish on both sides with seasoned fry mix; coat well.

Frying: In one deep-fry pot, fry fish, a few pieces at a time, until golden brown and crisp (about 2 to 3 minutes). In other deep-fry pot, fry potatoes, in small batches, until golden brown and crisp. Remove fish and potatoes from oil and drain on paper towels. Salt to taste; serve hot.

Makes 8 to 10 servings

For finicky family members who don't like fish,
substitute chicken tenders for the catfish.

Crawfish Egg Rolls

Jo Ann Anthony
Harahan, Louisiana
1996 Wesson Cookers' Club Recipe Contest Winner

2 tablespoons Wesson® Vegetable Oil
2 (8-ounce) bags shredded cabbage mix *or* 1 pound napa
    cabbage, shredded
½ pound bean sprouts, washed and drained
2 teaspoons seasoned salt
1½ teaspoons garlic powder
1 pound seasoned crawfish tails, plus juices
½ cup LaChoy® Lite Soy Sauce
    Wesson® Vegetable Oil
1 (16-ounce) package egg roll/spring roll wrappers
    (20 count)

In large skillet, heat *2 tablespoons* Wesson Oil. Add cabbage and bean sprouts; sauté until tender. While vegetables are sautéing, add seasoned salt and garlic powder. Fold in crawfish with their juices and soy sauce; sauté 2 minutes more. Drain liquid thoroughly from mixture. Fill a large deep-fry pot or electric skillet to half its depth with Wesson Oil. Heat oil to 350°F. Meanwhile, place *⅓ cup* filling into *each* egg roll wrapper. Roll according to package directions. Working in small batches, fry egg rolls, turning once. Remove from oil and drain on paper towels.

Makes 20 egg rolls

Be creative with egg roll fillings. Try sausage,
shrimp or even corned beef and cabbage.

🕐 *Snappy Shrimp Zingers*

2 cups finely chopped cooked, shelled shrimp
½ cup all-purpose flour
3 tablespoons finely chopped green onion
3 tablespoons finely chopped red bell pepper
1 tablespoon minced fresh parsley
3 teaspoons fresh lemon juice
2¼ teaspoons Gebhardt® Hot Pepper Sauce
2 teaspoons Cajun seasoning
½ teaspoon salt
1 egg, slightly beaten
1 cup fine dry bread crumbs
2 cups Wesson® Canola Oil

In medium bowl, combine *first 9* ingredients, ending with salt; blend well. Add egg and blend until thoroughly combined. (Mixture will be sticky.) Shape mixture into 12 (3×¾-inch) stick-shaped pieces. Gently roll *each* piece in bread crumbs. In a large skillet, heat oil to 325°F. Gently place shrimp sticks into oil and fry until crisp and golden brown. Drain on paper towels. Serve with your favorite dipping sauce or a squeeze of lemon.

Makes about 12 zingers

🕐 *Vala's Finest Corn Fritters*

Wesson® Vegetable Oil
2 eggs, beaten
½ cup milk
1 (7-ounce) can whole kernel corn, drained
2 cups self-rising flour
Sifted powdered sugar

Fill a deep-fry pot or heavy stockpot to half its depth with Wesson Oil. Heat oil to 350°F to 375°F. Meanwhile, in a large mixing bowl, whisk together the eggs and milk; stir in corn. Add the flour; mix gently until just moistened. Using an ice cream scoop or a ¼ cup measure, form the dough into balls; place on waxed paper. Let stand for 10 minutes. Fry until dark golden brown (about 10 to 15 minutes). Remove and drain on paper towels. Sprinkle generously with powdered sugar. Serve hot with syrup or honey, if desired.

Makes 8 to 10 servings

Desserts

*From sweet and light to rich and gooey, these recipes
are the happy ending to your perfect meal.*

Brandied Peach Cobbler

Filling:
  6 cups fresh sliced peaches (3 pounds) *or* 2 (16-ounce)
    packages frozen sliced peaches
  ½ cup sugar
  ¼ cup brandy
  1 tablespoon corn starch
  1 tablespoon fresh lemon juice
  1 teaspoon brandy extract
  ½ teaspoon cinnamon
    Wesson® No-Stick Cooking Spray

Topping:
  1 cup all-purpose flour
  ⅔ cup sugar
  1 tablespoon baking powder
  1 teaspoon cinnamon
  ½ teaspoon salt
  ½ cup Wesson® Vegetable Oil
  ¼ cup milk
  ½ cup chopped pecans
    Homemade vanilla ice cream

continued on page 82

Brandied Peach Cobbler

Brandied Peach Cobbler, continued

Filling: In a large bowl, combine *all* filling ingredients *except* Wesson Cooking Spray. Let stand 30 minutes, stirring often. Meanwhile, preheat oven to 375°F and spray an 11×7×2-inch baking dish with Wesson Cooking Spray.

Topping: In a medium bowl, combine flour, sugar, baking powder, cinnamon and salt; mix well. Add Wesson Oil and milk; blend well. Fold in pecans. Pour peach mixture into baking dish. Evenly drop topping mixture by rounded tablespoons over peach mixture. Bake 45 to 55 minutes or until brown and bubbly. Serve cold or at room temperature with homemade vanilla ice cream.   *Makes 6 servings*

Lena's Famous Pecan Pie

    1 unbaked (9-inch) Stir-n-Roll Pie Crust (page 83)
    1 cup packed dark brown sugar
    4 eggs, beaten
    ¼ cup light corn syrup
    ¼ cup molasses
    3 teaspoons vanilla
    ½ teaspoon salt
       Grated peel from one lemon or orange
    ¼ cup Wesson® Vegetable Oil
    1½ tablespoons cornstarch
    1½ cups chopped pecans
    1¼ cups perfect pecan halves
       Homemade vanilla ice cream or whipped cream

Prepare Stir-n-Roll Pie Crust; set aside.

Preheat oven to 375°F. In large bowl, combine *next* 7 ingredients, ending with lemon peel; blend well. In small bowl, stir together Wesson Oil and cornstarch until cornstarch is completely dissolved. Pour oil mixture into sugar mixture; mix well. Stir in chopped pecans. Pour pie filling into pie crust. Arrange pecan halves over filling. Bake for 30 minutes. Cover pie with foil and continue baking an additional 30 minutes. Cool pie completely (at least 3 hours) before serving. Top with ice cream or whipped cream.   *Makes 8 servings*

Peanut Brittle Pie

1 unbaked (9-inch) Stir-n-Roll Pie Crust (recipe follows)
1 cup beer nuts
3 eggs, at room temperature
3 tablespoons cornstarch
1 cup firmly packed light brown sugar
3 tablespoons Wesson® Corn Oil
1 cup maple syrup
1 teaspoon maple extract
1 teaspoon vanilla extract

Prepare Stir-n-Roll Pie Crust. Sprinkle bottom of crust with ½ *cup* nuts; set aside *remaining* nuts.

Preheat oven to 450°F. In a medium bowl, whisk eggs until foamy. In another medium bowl, gradually add egg mixture to cornstarch; mix well. Add brown sugar and Wesson Oil; blend well. Stir in maple syrup and extracts; mix well. Pour filling into nut-covered pie shell. Sprinkle *remaining* nuts on top. Bake at 450°F for 15 minutes. Lower oven temperature to 350°F and continue baking for 30 minutes or until center has set. *Do not over bake.*   *Makes 8 servings*

 # Stir-n-Roll Pie Crust

1½ cups sifted all-purpose flour
 ¾ teaspoon salt
 ⅓ cup Wesson® Vegetable Oil
 ¼ cup ice water

In a medium bowl, mix flour and salt. Add Wesson Oil and water all at once to flour. With a fork, stir until mixture holds together. Shape dough into a ball and flatten. Roll between two pieces of waxed paper to a 12-inch diameter. Peel off one piece of paper and invert dough, paper side up, into 9-inch pie plate. Peel off second piece of paper. Ease and fit pastry into plate; trim and flute edges.

Without filling: Completely pierce bottom and sides of pie crust with fork. Bake at 425°F for 12 minutes or until golden brown.

With filling: Do not pierce pie crust. Fill as desired and bake according to pie recipe.

Double Crusted Pie: Double the recipe and follow the same preparation method. Evenly divide dough before rolling out into pie pans.
                                                        Makes 1 (9-inch) pie crust

Cranapple Pan-Fried Skillet Cake

Cake:
    Wesson® No-Stick Cooking Spray
2½ cups peeled, cored and sliced apples
  1 (16-ounce) can whole cranberry sauce
  3 tablespoons melted butter
  ¾ cup firmly packed light brown sugar
  ½ cup walnut pieces
  2 cups all-purpose flour
1⅓ cups granulated sugar
  2 teaspoons baking powder
  ½ teaspoon salt
  ½ cup Wesson® Vegetable Oil
  ¼ cup milk
  1 egg
  3 tablespoons fresh orange juice
1½ tablespoons grated fresh orange peel (2 oranges)
  1 teaspoon vanilla

Topping:
    Remaining ½ can whole cranberry sauce
  2 tablespoons fresh orange juice
  1 tablespoon Wesson® Vegetable Oil
    Walnut pieces for garnish

Cake: Generously spray an 11-inch skillet with straight sides with Wesson Cooking Spray. Place apples in pan in a single layer. Spoon *half* the can of cranberry sauce evenly on and around apples; reserve *remaining* cranberry sauce. Drizzle apples with butter and sprinkle with brown sugar and walnuts. Set aside. In a large bowl, combine flour, sugar, baking powder and salt; blend well. Add *next 6* ingredients, ending with vanilla. With an electric mixer, on LOW speed, beat 2 minutes until moistened and then an additional 2 minutes on HIGH, scraping bowl often. Carefully pour batter evenly over fruit mixture in skillet. Cover skillet and place on range top over LOW heat for 1 hour or until wooden pick inserted into center comes out clean. Cut around edges of skillet to loosen cake and invert onto serving plate. (Leave any fruit that sticks to the skillet; it may be combined with the topping ingredients.)

Topping: Add topping ingredients except walnuts to skillet; heat through. Spread quickly over warm cake and top with walnuts, if desired.

Makes 8 servings

Ooey Gooey Peanut Butter and Fudge Brownies

Batter:
  Wesson® No-Stick Cooking Spray
  3 cups sugar
  1 cup (2 sticks) butter, softened
  ½ cup Wesson® Vegetable Oil
  1 tablespoon plus 1½ teaspoons vanilla
  6 eggs, at room temperature
2¼ cups all-purpose flour
1¼ cups cocoa
1½ teaspoons baking powder
  ¾ teaspoon salt
  1 (10-ounce) bag peanut butter chips

Filling:
1½ cups PETER PAN® Creamy Peanut Butter
  ⅓ cup Wesson® Vegetable Oil
  ½ cup sugar
  3 tablespoons all-purpose flour
  3 eggs, at room temperature
  1 tablespoon vanilla

Frosting:
  3 (1-ounce) bars unsweetened chocolate
  3 tablespoons PETER PAN® Creamy Peanut Butter
2⅔ cups powdered sugar
  ¼ cup water
  1 teaspoon vanilla
  ¼ teaspoon salt

Batter: Preheat oven to 350°F. Spray two 13×9×2-inch baking pans with Wesson Cooking Spray. In a large bowl, beat sugar and butter until creamy. Add Wesson Oil and vanilla. Add eggs, one at a time, beating well after *each* addition. In a small bowl, combine flour, cocoa, baking powder and salt; blend well. While beating, gradually add flour mixture to creamed mixture; mix well. Fold in peanut butter chips. Evenly spread ¼ of batter into 1 pan.

continued on page 88

*Ooey Gooey Peanut Butter
and Fudge Brownies*

Ooey Gooey Peanut Butter and Fudge Brownies, continued

Filling: In a small bowl, cream together Peter Pan Peanut Butter and Wesson Oil. Add sugar and flour; blend well. Add eggs and vanilla; beat until smooth. Carefully spread ½ of filling mixture evenly over batter in pan. Top filling with an additional ¼ of batter and spread evenly. Gently cut through layers to create a marble effect throughout the brownies. Repeat process with *remaining* pan and *remaining* batter and *remaining* filling. Bake for 30 minutes. *Do not over bake.*

Frosting: Meanwhile, in a medium saucepan, melt chocolate and peanut butter over LOW heat, stirring constantly. Remove from heat and stir in *remaining* ingredients; mix until smooth. If frosting is too thick, add an additional 1 to 3 tablespoons of water. Spread frosting over brownies **immediately** after baking. Cool in pans on wire racks.

Makes 3 dozen brownies

Southern Belle
White Chocolate Cookies

½ cup **PETER PAN**® **Creamy Peanut Butter**
¼ cup **Wesson**® **Vegetable Oil**
¼ cup (½ stick) butter
½ cup granulated sugar
½ cup firmly packed brown sugar
1 egg, at room temperature, slightly beaten
2 teaspoons vanilla
½ teaspoon baking soda
½ teaspoon baking powder
1¼ cups all-purpose flour
2 (4-ounce) bars white confection candy bar for baking
    and eating
1⅓ cups coarsely chopped macadamia nuts

Preheat oven to 350°F. In a large mixing bowl, using an electric mixer, beat Peter Pan Peanut Butter, Wesson Oil and butter together until creamy. Add *next 6* ingredients, ending with baking powder; beat on MEDIUM speed until well blended. Add flour and continue mixing until well blended. Keeping candy bars in wrappers, hit bars against counter to break them into small chunks. Fold candy chunks and nuts into cookie dough. Place heaping tablespoons of dough onto an ungreased cookie sheet 1½ inches apart, pressing dough down slightly with the back of spoon. Bake 10 to 12 minutes or until lightly brown around edges. Remove from cookie sheet; cool on wire rack.

Makes 15 cookies

Bread Pudding

¾ **cup raisins**
¼ **cup whiskey or bourbon**
   Wesson® No-Stick Cooking Spray
10 **cups stale bread, biscuits, muffins, etc.**
 1 **cup half-and-half**
 1 **cup milk**
 1 **cup granulated sugar**
½ **cup firmly packed brown sugar**
 3 **eggs**
1½ **tablespoons vanilla**
½ **teaspoon cinnamon**
¼ **cup Wesson® Vegetable Oil**
   Homemade vanilla ice cream or whiskey sauce

Soak raisins in whiskey at least 2 hours or overnight. Preheat oven to 325°F. Spray 11×7×2-inch baking dish with Wesson Cooking Spray. In a large bowl, combine bread, raisin mixture and *remaining* ingredients *except* ice cream or whiskey sauce. Toss slightly; let stand 10 minutes to allow bread to soak. Spoon bread mixture into prepared dish; bake for 50 to 60 minutes or until very firm. Cool; serve with homemade vanilla ice cream or your favorite whiskey sauce.   *Makes 8 to 10 servings*

Rich & Gooey Apple-Caramel Cake

Cake:
   Wesson® No-Stick Cooking Spray
  2 cups all-purpose flour
  1 teaspoon salt
  1 teaspoon baking soda
  1 teaspoon pumpkin pie spice
1½ cups sugar
  ¾ cup Wesson® Vegetable Oil
  3 eggs
  2 teaspoons vanilla
  3 cups peeled, cored and sliced tart apples, such as Granny
     Smith, ½-inch slices
  1 cup chopped walnuts

Glaze:
  1 cup firmly packed light brown sugar
  ½ cup (1 stick) butter
  ¼ cup milk
     Whipped cream

Cake: Preheat oven to 350°F. Spray a 13×9×2-inch baking pan with
Wesson Cooking Spray; set aside. In medium bowl, combine flour, salt,
baking soda and pie spice; mix well. Set aside. In large bowl, with
electric mixer, beat sugar, Wesson Oil, eggs and vanilla for 3 minutes at
MEDIUM speed. Add flour mixture and stir until dry ingredients are
moistened; fold in apples and walnuts. Pour batter into baking pan and
spread evenly; bake 50 to 55 minutes or until wooden pick inserted
into center comes out clean. Cool cake in pan on wire rack.

Glaze: Meanwhile, in small saucepan over MEDIUM heat, bring brown
sugar, butter and milk to a boil, stirring until sugar has dissolved. Boil 1
minute. Spoon *half* of glaze over warm cake; set *remaining* aside.
Allow cake to stand 5 minutes. Top each serving with *remaining* glaze
and whipped cream.   *Makes 12 to 15 servings*

Strawberry Nut Cake

Sarah R. Scott
Charlotte, North Carolina
1996 Wesson Cookers' Club Recipe Contest Winner

Cake:
   Wesson® No-Stick Cooking Spray
 1 (1-pound 2¼-ounce) box white cake mix
 1 (3-ounce) box strawberry gelatin
 ¾ cup Wesson® Vegetable or Canola Oil
 ½ cup milk
 4 eggs, beaten
 1 cup fresh sliced strawberries or 1 cup thawed and
    drained frozen sliced strawberries

Icing:
 ¼ cup (½ stick) butter or margarine, softened
 2 cups powdered sugar, sifted
 ½ cup fresh chopped strawberries
 ½ cup chopped pecans

Cake: Preheat oven to 350°F. Spray a 13×9×2-inch baking dish with Wesson Cooking Spray. In a large mixing bowl, combine cake mix, gelatin, Wesson Oil, milk and eggs. Using an electric mixer on HIGH speed, beat ingredients for 2 minutes. Gently fold strawberries into batter; blend well. Pour batter into baking dish. Bake for 30 to 35 minutes or until wooden pick inserted into center comes out clean; cool.

Icing: While cake is cooling, mix together butter and sugar until smooth. If too thin, add more sifted sugar until desired icing consistency is reached. Fold in strawberries and pecans. Gently spread icing over cake.   *Makes 10 servings*

Sarah loves to serve this cake as the finale to her family's favorite meal: fried pork chops, stir-fried vegetables and green salad with homemade dressing.

Index